THE HEART'S ECHOES OF ODES TO JESUS

MY HEART'S WHISPERS

RACHEL A CHRISTOPHER

Copyright © Rachel A Christopher
All Rights Reserved.

This book has been self-published with all reasonable efforts taken to make the material error-free by the author. No part of this book shall be used, reproduced in any manner whatsoever without written permission from the author, except in the case of brief quotations embodied in critical articles and reviews.

The Author of this book is solely responsible and liable for its content including but not limited to the views, representations, descriptions, statements, information, opinions and references ["Content"]. The Content of this book shall not constitute or be construed or deemed to reflect the opinion or expression of the Publisher or Editor. Neither the Publisher nor Editor endorse or approve the Content of this book or guarantee the reliability, accuracy or completeness of the Content published herein and do not make any representations or warranties of any kind, express or implied, including but not limited to the implied warranties of merchantability, fitness for a particular purpose. The Publisher and Editor shall not be liable whatsoever for any errors, omissions, whether such errors or omissions result from negligence, accident, or any other cause or claims for loss or damages of any kind, including without limitation, indirect or consequential loss or damage arising out of use, inability to use, or about the reliability, accuracy or sufficiency of the information contained in this book.

Made with ♥ on the Notion Press Platform
www.notionpress.com

DEDICATION:

This is to You, my precious Jesus.
From calling me to a purpose still unfolding, to using me—little by
little—for Your glory in ways I never imagined.
A simple token of gratitude for You, my love.
I pray it points hearts back to You.

Contents

Acknowledgements

"First, thank You, God, for never letting me walk alone and for filling my heart with hope every step of the way. To my bestie, a true gift from God—thank you for your endless encouragement and for believing in me even when I doubted myself. To my sister, I'll always love you—your strength and love inspire me every day. To my beautiful mother, your unwavering support and prayers have been my foundation. To my father, who made me bold to aim for much greater, thank you for your guidance. To my charming brother, thank you for your constant support and curious spirit—it kept me going and made the journey lighter. And to my supportive friends, your kindness and cheer have lifted me up in countless ways. This book is a testament to your love and belief in me. I couldn't have done this without each of you."

ACKNOWLEDGEMENTS

Foreword

When I first read Rachel's words, I wasn't just reading poetry—I was listening to a heart in deep conversation with God. The Heart's Echoes of Odes to Jesus is more than a collection of poems; it is a sacred journey through vulnerability, brokenness, healing, and the unrelenting love of Jesus.Rachel writes with such honesty and grace that her words don't just sit on the page—they reach out and hold your hand. I've watched her pour not just ink, but pieces of her soul into these lines. And in doing so, she's created a space where anyone who has ever felt lost, hurt, or yearning for something greater can find comfort and hope.This book is a testament to what happens when faith meets creativity, when pain is transformed into praise, and when one heart dares to whisper what many feel but can't always express.To the reader: may these poems stir something in you—may they echo in your own heart, pointing you to the unwavering love of Christ.

    With love and admiration,

Annie Ruth.

Preface

I wrote this book because I felt a deep calling to write about His love. What began as a single ode has now blossomed into a collection meant to uplift readers and invite them to experience the same Jesus whose love has changed my heart. Through these poems, I hope to share not just my faith but a heartfelt longing to connect and find hope in Him.

This is more than poetry—it's a journey of love, struggle, and grace. I pray that these words resonate with you and bring you closer to the gentle presence of Jesus.

Prologue

From the very first light of a new day dawning,

To the final breath of my mortal life's journey,

Let my love for You be an exquisite painting—

Your will and mine in heavenly harmony.

Jesus, make me a lover of Thine;

Help me make You the sole desire of mine.

1. LORD, YOUR LOVE FOR ME

"Oh Lord, this love you have for me,
Unfathomable, how can it ever be?
Even the shadow of your love, I am unworthy of,
But you gave your own life on my behalf.
Life goes around me in circles ,
But from afar, I see your love,
Like a little hope of light that twinkles.
Even while afar, your love calls unto me ,
"Come to me, my little one, why do you fumble?"
How, Lord, can I ever comprehend,
How your love for me knows no end?"

2. TO YOU OH LORD, I BELONG

"*To You, Oh Lord, I belong,*
To You, who put in me a new song.
My safest place is under Your wings, Oh!
And to think of that, what joy it brings!
I run to You in times of trouble;
How You receive me with open arms is like no other.
In Your arms, Lord, I long to be;
Forever, let this be my only plea.
Where, Lord, is my rest and peace?
Is it not Your precious Word that brings me to ease?
My desire is this, Lord: to seek You earnestly,
And to rejoice in only You abundantly."

3. DEAR LILY OF THE VALLEY

Dear Lily of the valley,
With humility and grace , Yourself , You carry .
You rejuvenate the bees with Your sweetness;
And Your dainty leaves sing greatly of your comeliness.
You boast not of the beauty you assume,
Nor of the rich scent of your perfume!
You grow, seeking no light or fame,
Yet amongst them all, you bear the loveliest name!
Most beautiful among the flowers in the valley,
Is , Jesus, the Lily of the Valley!

4. HIS RICHNESS IN HUMILITY

The brightest of the stars , even the sun ,
Shys away before the majestic glory of the Son .
Your eyes are on the ones with an untold story ,
Whom you're willing to call for the purpose of your glory .
I may not possess anything worthy of praise;
But for the redemption of my sins ,from death you were raised !
I can never be perfect,though I may try,
Still I'm Your child, that You will never deny .
Lord, I know one thing for sure,
That I yearn to behold your beauty forevermore.

• 8 •

THE HEART'S ECHOES OF ODES TO JESUS

5. JESUS, MY GUIDING LIGHT

Walking down the darkest alleys,
Burden of my sin upon me I carry;
I know not the way I need to go,
And I had no hope of a happy morrow.
But then came Jesus, my guiding light,
Poured into my heart His joy and delight!
My burdens upon Himself, He bore,
And led me towards a future sure!
Jesus, You're my guiding light;
And to walk with You is forever my joy and delight!

6. SHADES OF JESUS

Golden yellow was His face that shone ;
Worthy of all praise was this man alone !
Blue ocean-like was his calmness and peace ;
Even though was made a subject of mockery and tease .
Crimson was every drop of Blood He shed ;
Humbly bore the shame when as captive He was led .
Whiter than the snow is He , Who rose up from the dead;
Good news He now gives for you and me to spread !

7. YOUR PRECIOUS WORD

It's your Word, Lord, that giveth life.
It's your Word that rids all strife.
It's your Word that draws me nigh
To the Saviour above, Who's seated on high.
In your word my trust I puteth,
It gives hope to the soul that seeketh.
The grass withers, and the flowers fade,
But the Word of the Lord ever remains!

• 14 •

THE HEART'S ECHOES OF ODES TO JESUS

8. HE KNOWS ALL SEASONS

In His time, He makes it all right,
And in His time, He makes life beautiful and bright.
He knows when storms of life can knock you down,
But holds in store an everlasting crown.
To wait upon the Lord renews the despaired heart's glee,
And to find rest in His presence is like a calmed turbulent sea.
So trust in the Lord with all your heart;
Leaning not on your own understanding makes life a sweet art.
Verily verily I say to unto you,
Trust in the Lord with all your heart!
A gentle reminder i wish to impart .

9. THE BLESSINGS OF THE LORD

As the dew drops gently fall by the morning's dawn,
The flowers rejoice over their dwindling forlorn;
Like the rain that washes the earth's long grieving,
And leaves all creation to celebrate their renewing.
So are the blessings of the Lord upon His people and land,
Rewarding each of them for the work of their hands.
Blessed are the people of the Lord;
They are like the trees planted by the rivers,
Flourishing forever in the presence of the Giver

10. THE POTTER'S HANDIWORK

Void of worth, the fragments lay bare,
Weeping in agony, with no joy to share.
It asketh, "What future holds this futile clay?"
"Beauty and honour," the Potter doth say.
With gentleness, He moldeth with whispers of care,
His tender hands ne'er grew weary til' it be yare.
It was once clay, trodden on the way,
Now, a chalice of honour, in the Potter's display!

11. MY LORD-MY VICTORY

As Sorrow departs, hailing its "victory",
the joy of the Lord imparts a different story.
The Lord bestows and takes away.
My soul remains steadfast, come what may.
Though the armies of uncertainty march towards me,
my soul quivers not, for the Lion of Judah goes before me!
My victory comes from Him, my Lord,
My heart sings praises with cymbals in joyful chord!

12. MY PRAYER FOR THE READERS

Dear Lord Jesus, as readers embark on this journey through my book, I humbly pray that Your presence touches their hearts and lives. May they discover the depth of Your love and find purpose in Your plan for them. I pray that they feel Your unwavering love, no matter the trials or triumphs they face. May Your love overflow in their lives, bringing joy, peace, and guidance. Bless this book, Lord, and may it be a blessing unto my readers. In the precious name of Jesus Christ, I pray. Amen.

A Gentle Reminder

"But seek ye first the kingdom of God, and his righteousness; and all these things shall be added unto you." - Matthew 6:33

"The Lord bless you
and keep you; the Lord make his face shine on you
and be gracious to you; the Lord turn his face toward you
and give you peace."
Numbers 6:24-26

www.ingramcontent.com/pod-product-compliance
Lightning Source LLC
Chambersburg PA
CBHW020518160726
47991CB00007B/3011